NATURE'S SUPERHEROES

# SUPER
# CHAMELEONS

by Karen Latchana Kenney

pogo

# Ideas for Parents and Teachers

Pogo Books let children practice reading informational text while introducing them to nonfiction features such as headings, labels, sidebars, maps, and diagrams, as well as a table of contents, glossary, and index.

Carefully leveled text with a strong photo match offers early fluent readers the support they need to succeed.

## Before Reading

- "Walk" through the book and point out the various nonfiction features. Ask the student what purpose each feature serves.

- Look at the glossary together. Read and discuss the words.

## Read the Book

- Have the child read the book independently.

- Invite him or her to list questions that arise from reading.

## After Reading

- Discuss the child's questions. Talk about how he or she might find answers to those questions.

- Prompt the child to think more. Ask: What did you know about chameleons before you read this book? What more do you want to learn after reading it?

Pogo Books are published by Jump!
5357 Penn Avenue South
Minneapolis, MN 55419
www.jumplibrary.com

Library of Congress Cataloging-in-Publication Data

Names: Kenney, Karen Latchana. author.
Title: Super chameleons / by Karen Latchana Kenney.
Description: Minneapolis, MN: Jump!, Inc., [2018]
Series: Nature's superheroes | Audience: Ages 7-10.
Includes bibliographical references and index.
Identifiers: LCCN 2017029249 (print)
LCCN 2017027722 (ebook)
ISBN 9781624967078 (ebook)
ISBN 9781620319673 (hardcover: alk. paper)
ISBN 9781620319680 (pbk.)
Subjects: LCSH: Chameleons—Juvenile literature.
Classification: LCC QL666.L23 (print)
LCC QL666.L23 K47 2017 (ebook) | DDC 597.95/6—dc23
LC record available at https://lccn.loc.gov/2017029249

Editor: Jenna Trnka
Book Designer: Michelle Sonnek
Photo Researcher: Michelle Sonnek

Photo Credits: Eric Isselee/Shutterstock, cover, 3, 8, 23; Nikiforov Volodymyr/Shutterstock, 1; Gandee Vasan/Getty, 4; dave stamboulis/Alamy, 5; Dr. Alexandra Laube/imageBROKER/SuperStock, 6-7; Giovanni Giuseppe Bellani/Alamy, 9; Cathy Keifer/Shutterstock, 10-11; blickwinkel/SuperStock, 12-13; Nick Henn/Shutterstock, 14; Jan Bures/Shutterstock, 15; FLPA/SuperStock, 16-17 (foreground); Lenor Ko/Shutterstock, 16-17 (background); NHPA/SuperStock, 18-19; ABD/Getty, 20-21.

Printed in the United States of America at Corporate Graphics in North Mankato, Minnesota.

# TABLE OF CONTENTS

# CHAPTER 1

······································

# LIFE IN THE TREES

What animal's tongue shoots out faster than a race car drives? What can see the sky and the ground at the same time? And what creature can change colors?

This captain of color
has incredible powers.
It's a chameleon!

Most chameleons live in Madagascar and other parts of Africa. Many have long tails that curl. Chameleons climb high in the trees. They use their tail and clawlike feet to grip branches.

**DID YOU KNOW?**

There are more than 180 kinds of chameleons. The tiniest can fit on a match head.

# CHAPTER 2
## SUPER CHAMELEON SKILLS

Chameleons have super eyesight. Their unique eyes dart everywhere. They can move in almost a complete circle.

Each eye moves separately. One eye looks up. At the same time, the other can look down. To really focus, a chameleon points both eyes in the same direction.

Chameleons are slow. But their tongues are incredibly fast. At the end is a ball of muscle. It is sticky. The tongue shoots out. It sticks to the **prey**. Then the chameleon quickly pulls its tongue back along with the bug.

## DID YOU KNOW?

A chameleon has a long tongue to snag food. It can reach two times the lizard's body length.

tongue

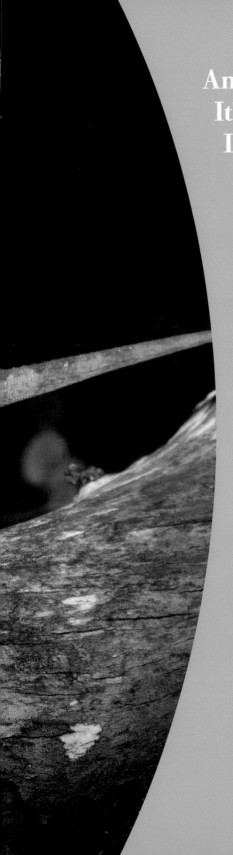

Another skill looks like a dance. It's the way this lizard walks. It lifts one arm and one leg. It sways back and forth. This **mimics** leaves moving in the wind. It takes a step. It starts its dance again. It helps chameleons hide from **predators**.

# CHAPTER 3

# CAPTAINS OF COLOR

What is the chameleon's most unique skill? It can change colors! Chameleons are green or brown most of the time. But that can change in a flash.

How? Special skin cells. The cells are filled with different colors. They also have **crystals**. These **reflect** different colors. The colors and crystals help the skin change.

Green. Blue. Red. These colors don't just look pretty. They help chameleons. A chameleon can change its color to change its body **temperature**. If it is cold, it becomes darker. Dark colors absorb more sunlight. This warms the chameleon. If it is too hot, the lizard turns lighter. Lighter colors reflect sunlight. This keeps the chameleon cool.

# TAKE A LOOK!

A chameleon has many features that make it one of nature's superheroes!

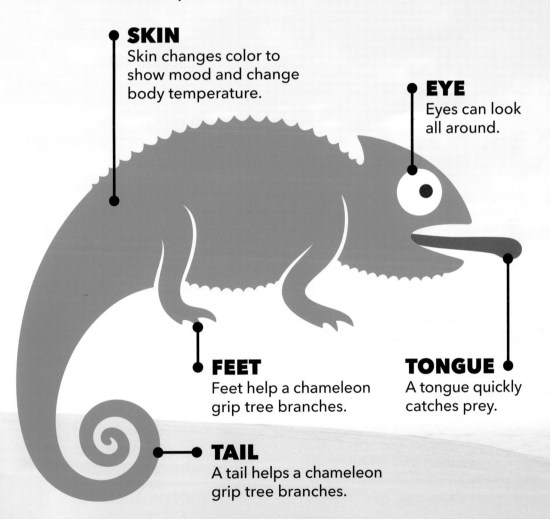

**SKIN**
Skin changes color to show mood and change body temperature.

**EYE**
Eyes can look all around.

**FEET**
Feet help a chameleon grip tree branches.

**TONGUE**
A tongue quickly catches prey.

**TAIL**
A tail helps a chameleon grip tree branches.

But there's more to a chameleon's color. It's a way of talking. A chameleon's color tells **mates** to come near or go away. It can show anger, strength, or fear.

**DID YOU KNOW?**

Some people think chameleons change color to match their environment. But that is a **myth**.

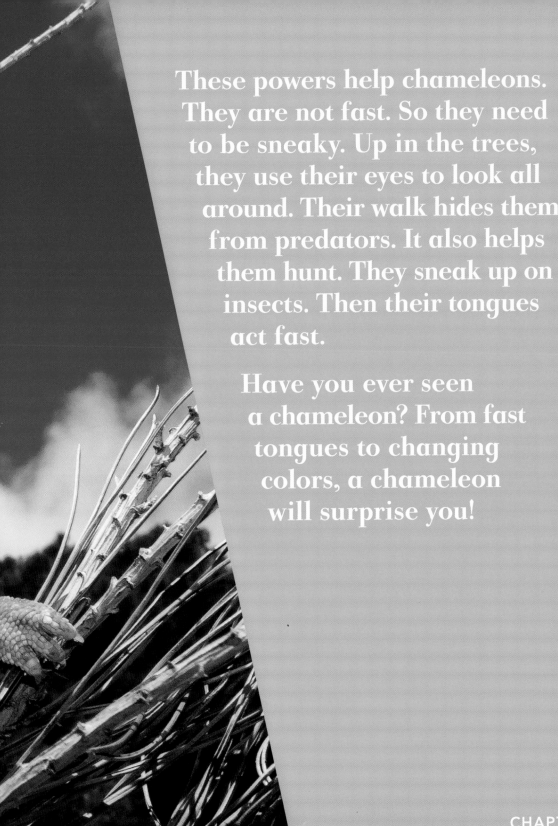

These powers help chameleons. They are not fast. So they need to be sneaky. Up in the trees, they use their eyes to look all around. Their walk hides them from predators. It also helps them hunt. They sneak up on insects. Then their tongues act fast.

Have you ever seen a chameleon? From fast tongues to changing colors, a chameleon will surprise you!

# ACTIVITIES & TOOLS

## HOT OR COLD?

Chameleons can change color to warm or cool their bodies. See how color affects temperature with this activity!

**What You Need:**
- 2 glasses that are the same
- water
- thermometer
- white paper
- black paper
- 2 rubber bands
- notebook
- pencil
- sunlight

1. Pour the same amount of water into each glass.

2. Wrap the black paper around a glass. Hold it in place with a rubber band.

3. Wrap the white paper around the other glass. Hold it in place with a rubber band.

4. Put the thermometer in a glass. Wait a minute and then look at the thermometer. Record the temperature. Repeat with the other glass.

5. Put both glasses out in the sunlight for a few hours.

6. Take the temperature of the water in each glass. Record your results. Are they different? Which one is warmer?

# GLOSSARY

**crystals:** Solid substances that reflect light.

**mates:** Male and female partners that reproduce.

**mimics:** Copies the actions of something else.

**myth:** A widely believed idea that is actually false.

**predators:** Animals that hunt other animals for food.

**prey:** An animal that is hunted by another animal for food.

**reflect:** To bounce back light rays.

**temperature:** The amount of heat in something.

## INDEX

## TO LEARN MORE

Learning more is as easy as 1, 2, 3.

1) Go to www.factsurfer.com

2) Enter "superchameleons" into the search box.

3) Click the "Surf" button to see a list of websites.

With factsurfer, finding more information is just a click away.